BROO... ...

GUIDE 2024

Discover the Heartbeat of New York: A
Comprehensive Travel Guide to Brooklyn's
Vibrant Culture, Iconic Landmarks, and Local
Treasures

Donald M. Clark

Table Of Content

Chapter 1: Introduction to Brooklyn

Overview of Brooklyn's History and Culture

Brooklyn, one of New York City's five boroughs, has a rich and diverse past that has molded its distinct culture. Brooklyn has seen considerable modifications since its early Dutch colonization in the 17th century to its current status as a lively and prosperous municipality. This overview will go into the major historical events and cultural components that have led to Brooklyn's growth.

Brooklyn's history may be traced back to the early 17th century when it was inhabited by the Lenape Native American tribe. The Dutch West India Company built a trading facility in Breuckelen, which later became Brooklyn, in 1636. The Dutch influence can still be observed in some Brooklyn neighborhood names, such as Flatbush and Bushwick.

Brooklyn was crucial throughout the American Revolution. The Battle of Long Island, which took place in what is now Prospect Park in August 1776, resulted in a British triumph. George Washington's strategic retreat, on the other hand, allowed his forces to reorganize and continue fighting for freedom.

Brooklyn saw tremendous industry and urbanization in the nineteenth century. The Erie

Canal, completed in 1825, linked Brooklyn to the Great Lakes region, boosting trade and transportation. Industries including shipbuilding, sugar refining, and manufacturing thrived, bringing immigrants from all across Europe.

In 1883, the Brooklyn Bridge was built, significantly transforming the borough. This iconic monument linked Brooklyn and Manhattan, making transportation between the two boroughs easier. The bridge came to represent development and growth for both Brooklyn and New York City in general.

Brooklyn's cultural landscape is distinguished by its diversified population and thriving arts scene. Throughout its history, the borough has been a magnet for immigrants, resulting in a complex tapestry of cultures. Williamsburg, DUMBO

(Down Under the Manhattan Bridge Overpass), and Park Slope are well-known for their artistic communities, which draw artists, musicians, and authors.

Brooklyn also has several cultural institutes and sites. The Brooklyn Museum, first opened in 1895, holds a large collection of international art. The Brooklyn Academy of Music (BAM) is a world-class performing arts center that presents theater, dance, music, and film. Since the late 1800s, Coney Island, with its famed amusement park rides and boardwalk, has been a popular destination for both locals and tourists.

Brooklyn has experienced tremendous gentrification and regeneration in recent years. DUMBO and Brooklyn Heights have experienced an inflow of young professionals, which has resulted in the creation of trendy restaurants, boutiques, and art galleries. This development has brought both advantages and disadvantages to the local community since it has resulted in rising housing costs and concerns about retaining the borough's distinct character.

Brooklyn's history and culture are inextricably linked. Brooklyn has evolved, from its Dutch roots to its involvement in the American Revolution and subsequent industrialization. Its diversified population and thriving arts scene have contributed to its status as a cultural center. As the borough evolves and grows, it will always be a site where history meets contemporary.

Neighborhoods and Geography

Brooklyn, one of New York City's five boroughs, is located in the state of New York's southeastern region. It is located on Long Island's western tip, separated from Manhattan by the East River. Brooklyn's geography is diversified, including coastal areas, rivers, parks, and many neighborhoods, each having its distinct character and charm.

Brooklyn's Geography

Brooklyn is the second-largest borough in terms of land area, with an area of around 71 square miles (183 square kilometers). The East River to the west, the Upper New York Bay to the south, and the Lower New York Bay to the east surround it on three sides. The borough's shoreline runs for roughly 26 miles (42 kilometers) and provides breathtaking views of Manhattan.

In comparison to other regions of New York City, the landscape of Brooklyn is rather flat. There are a few significant exceptions, such as Prospect Park and Greenwood Cemetery, which are located on glacial moraines and hence have higher landscapes. These places provide stunning vistas and recreational activities for both residents and visitors.

Brooklyn's Neighborhoods

Brooklyn has a wide variety of neighborhoods, each with its own distinct personality and cultural background. Here are some notable Brooklyn neighborhoods:

Williamsburg

Williamsburg, located on the northern outskirts of Brooklyn, has become a popular neighborhood noted for its bustling arts scene, hipster culture, and thriving nightlife. It is made up of a combination of industrial structures, renovated lofts, and contemporary boutiques.

DUMBO

DUMBO, which stands for Down Under the Manhattan Bridge Overpass, is a waterfront area between the Manhattan and Brooklyn Bridges. It has stunning views of Manhattan and is well-known for its art galleries, expensive restaurants, and IT firms.

The Park Slope

Park Slope is a family-friendly neighborhood near Prospect Park known for its tree-lined avenues, historic brownstones, and vibrant commercial corridors. It has a diversified community and provides a variety of dining, shopping, and cultural opportunities.

Brooklyn Heights, New York

Brooklyn Heights is one of Brooklyn's oldest neighborhoods, known for its scenic streets and spectacular vistas of the Manhattan skyline. It is known for its exquisite brownstones, historic churches, and the world-famous Brooklyn Heights Promenade.

Coney Island, New York

Coney Island, located on the southern edge of Brooklyn, is a well-known coastal resort region noted for its amusement parks, boardwalk, and beach. It is a popular tourist and local site, especially during the summer months.

Aside from these dynamic neighborhoods, Brooklyn also includes Red Hook, Greenpoint, Bushwick, Bed-Stuy (Bedford-Stuyvesant), and many more. Each neighborhood has its distinct history, cultural institutions, parks, and attractions, all of which add to Brooklyn's overall diversity and liveliness.

Getting Around - Transportation Information

Brooklyn, one of New York City's five boroughs, is a bustling and diverse location with several transportation alternatives for both locals and visitors. Whether you're exploring the bustling streets of Downtown Brooklyn, taking in the gorgeous views of Brooklyn Bridge Park, or visiting cultural enclaves like Williamsburg or DUMBO, there are several forms of transportation to assist you get around the borough effectively.

Transportation by Public

Brooklyn has a well-developed public transit system, making it simple to travel within the borough and connect to other sections of New York City. The Metropolitan Transportation Authority (MTA) operates multiple subway lines and bus routes throughout Brooklyn, making transportation simple and economical. Brooklyn's subway system contains lines such as the A, C, F, G, and R trains, which service various parts of the city. Furthermore, many bus routes traverse Brooklyn, providing an additional form of transit for people who prefer to travel above ground.

Subway

In Brooklyn, the subway is frequently the favored form of transit for both inhabitants and tourists. It is a quick and efficient way to get from one community to another. The subway stations are conveniently positioned across the borough, and most lines have frequent service. Atlantic Avenue-Barclays Center, Jay Street-MetroTech, and Borough Hall are all important subway stations in Brooklyn. It is crucial to remember that owing to maintenance or schedule changes, subway service may vary late at night or on weekends.

Bus

Brooklyn's bus system is another dependable mode of transportation. The buses run a variety of routes that connect several borough neighborhoods and provide access to nearby locations. The bus stations are labeled with route numbers and destinations, making it simple to find the correct vehicle. For real-time bus schedules and route information, visit the MTA website or download a transport app.

Biking

Brooklyn has many bike lanes and pathways, making cycling a handy and pleasurable way to explore the borough. Citi Bike, a bike-sharing scheme, offers stations all across Brooklyn where you may borrow a bike for a short amount of time. This is an excellent choice for shorter outings or leisurely rides along the shore. There are also various bike rental companies in Brooklyn if you prefer to have your bike for an extended period.

Ferries

The waterfront location of Brooklyn allows for the use of ferries as a form of transportation. The NYC Ferry has various routes connecting

Brooklyn to other boroughs and locations including Manhattan, Queens, and Staten Island. The ferry service provides stunning views of the city skyline and is an excellent way to avoid traffic congestion. DUMBO, Greenpoint, and Red Hook are famous ferry terminals in Brooklyn.

Taxis and ride-sharing services

In Brooklyn, taxis and ridesharing services such as Uber and Lyft are freely available. On main streets or near popular neighborhoods, hailing a yellow taxi is quite simple. Ridesharing services allow you to reserve a car through a mobile app, providing a comfortable and dependable transportation choice. It's important to note that using these services during peak hours or in high-demand locations may result in surcharges.

Chapter 2: Must-Visit Attractions

Brooklyn Bridge and DUMBO

The Brooklyn Bridge and DUMBO (Down Under the Manhattan Bridge Overpass) are two prominent New York City icons that represent the borough of Brooklyn's rich history and vibrant culture. This thorough travel guide will tell you everything you need to know about visiting these locations, such as their history, architecture, neighboring attractions, and practical advice for a memorable trip.

The Brooklyn Bridge's History

The Brooklyn Bridge, built in 1883, is one of the country's oldest suspension bridges. John Augustus Roebling planned it, as did his son Washington Roebling, who oversaw its construction after his father died. The East River Bridge connects the boroughs of Manhattan and Brooklyn. It was originally designed to house horse-drawn carriages, pedestrians, and elevated trains. It is now an important transportation link for vehicles, cyclists, and pedestrians.

Brooklyn Bridge Architecture

The Brooklyn Bridge is famous for its outstanding architecture and engineering marvels. The suspension cables are supported by two Gothic-inspired stone towers. The main span of the bridge is 1,595 feet (486 meters), making it one of the world's largest suspension bridges at the time of its completion. The bridge's unusual arched form and sophisticated cable system add to its visual charm.

Crossing the Brooklyn Bridge

Walking across the Brooklyn Bridge is a popular tourist and local activity. The elevated pedestrian promenade over the traffic lanes provides stunning views of the Manhattan skyline, the East River, and the Statue of Liberty. The walkway has entrances on both sides of the bridge, near City Hall Park in Manhattan and Tillary Street in Brooklyn. Starting in Manhattan allows you to completely appreciate the panoramic views as you make your way towards Brooklyn.

DUMBO

DUMBO is a dynamic area recognized for its industrial heritage and creative dynamism, nestled beneath the Manhattan and Brooklyn Bridges. It has evolved from a manufacturing district to a trendy hub brimming with art galleries, shops, cafes, and tech firms. The cobblestone alleyways and converted warehouses of DUMBO lend it a special appeal that draws people from all over the world.

DUMBO attractions include

DUMBO has a wealth of sights and activities to offer visitors. The Brooklyn Bridge Park, a waterfront green space that spans along the East River, is one of the highlights. During the summer, it features breathtaking views of the Manhattan skyline, sports fields, playgrounds, and even a pop-up pool. Jane's Carousel, a wonderfully restored historic carousel that gives nostalgic delight to both children and adults, is another popular attraction.

DUMBO's Art and Culture

DUMBO is also known for its vibrant arts scene. Numerous art galleries in the area display works by both established and young artists. With its exhibitions, performances, and interactive installations, the annual DUMBO Arts Festival draws art lovers from all over the world. Furthermore, the St. Ann's Warehouse is a well-known performing arts theater that hosts a wide variety of theatrical plays.

DUMBO's Culinary Delights

Foodies will find something to eat when exploring DUMBO. The area is home to a variety of eateries with cuisines ranging from gourmet burgers to fine dining experiences. There's something for everyone, from handmade pizza at Grimaldi's to scrumptious pastries at Almondine Bakery.

Tips for Visiting the Brooklyn Bridge and DUMBO

- **Best Time to Visit:** While the Brooklyn Bridge and DUMBO are open all year, the spring and fall seasons provide great weather and less congestion.

- **Transportation:** City Hall (4, 5, 6) and High Street-Brooklyn Bridge (A, C) are the nearest subway stations to the

Brooklyn Bridge. DUMBO is accessible via the F rail or the East River Ferry.

- **Security:** When strolling across the Brooklyn Bridge, keep an eye out for bikers and stick to the designated pedestrian lane. Crossing roadways in DUMBO should be done with caution due to strong traffic.

- **Photography chances:** Both the Brooklyn Bridge and DUMBO offer wonderful photographic chances. Photograph the bridge from the pedestrian walkway, or explore DUMBO's lovely streets and shoreline for more angles.

- **Nearby Attractions:** After seeing the Brooklyn Bridge and DUMBO, consider visiting the Brooklyn Heights Promenade, which has panoramic views of Manhattan, or the New York Transit Museum, which is housed in a defunct subway station.

Brooklyn Botanic Garden and Prospect Park

Prospect Park and the Brooklyn Botanic Garden are two renowned attractions in the New York City borough of Brooklyn. These two sites allow visitors to discover nature, participate in recreational activities, and be immersed in the splendor of Brooklyn's natural spaces.

Prospect Park is a large public park covering 526 acres. It was created by Frederick Law Olmsted and Calvert Vaux, who are well-known for their work on Manhattan's Central Park. The park first opened in 1867 and has since become one of New York City's most renowned green spots.

Prospect Park's diversified terrain is one of its most notable aspects. The park contains a variety of open meadows, forests, and water bodies, which provide habitat for a variety of plant and animal species. Visitors can explore the park's numerous walking pathways and trails, which provide picturesque vistas and bird-watching possibilities. The Long Meadow in the park's center is a popular area for picnics and sporting activities.

The Brooklyn Botanic Garden is 52 acres in size and is located near Prospect Park. It was founded in 1910 to display a diverse range of plant species from around the world. The Japanese Hill-and-Pond landscape, the Cranford Rose Garden, and the Shakespeare Garden are among the themed gardens in the landscape.

One of the centerpieces of the Brooklyn Botanic Garden is the Japanese Hill-and-Pond Garden. It was the first Japanese-style garden established in a public garden in the United States, and it includes traditional components such as a pond, bridges, and stone lanterns. Over 5,000 rose bushes representing approximately 1,400 distinct types can be found at the Cranford Rose Garden. When the roses are in full bloom throughout the summer months, it is a breathtaking sight.

The Brooklyn Botanic Garden also offers several annual events that draw visitors from all over the world. The Cherry Blossom Festival, held in late April or early May when the garden's cherry trees are in full bloom, is one of the most popular events. The garden is converted into a sea of pink blossoms during this time, and cultural events and activities are organized to welcome the entrance of spring.

Prospect Park and the Brooklyn Botanic Garden both provide a variety of leisure opportunities for visitors. On designated trails in Prospect Park, visitors can enjoy cycling, rollerblading, or horseback riding. There are other sporting facilities for baseball, soccer, and tennis. Boating and fishing are permitted on the park's lake, and there is even a designated place for barbecues.

The Brooklyn Botanic Garden offers a peaceful setting for strolls and exploring. Visitors can take guided tours to learn more about the various plant types and their importance. The garden also provides educational programs and workshops for both adults and children on topics including gardening, horticulture, and conservation.

The Arts and Culture Scene in Williamsburg

Williamsburg, in the Brooklyn borough of New York, has grown as a thriving center for arts and culture. This neighborhood, known for its fashionable environment and creative spirit, has become a magnet for artists, musicians, and performers from all over the world. Williamsburg, with its broad assortment of galleries, theaters, music venues, and street art, provides a vibrant cultural experience that attracts both locals and tourists.

Galleries

Numerous art galleries in Williamsburg exhibit a diverse range of modern art. These galleries frequently host shows by both established and rising artists, allowing for artistic expression and experimentation. The MoMA PS1 is a renowned gallery in the neighborhood that focuses on modern art and offers a variety of exhibitions and activities throughout the year. Another notable gallery is the Pierogi Gallery, which is recognized for its diverse collection of artwork from various genres and mediums.

Public Art

The streets of Williamsburg are covered with bright murals and graffiti art, making it a sanctuary for street art fans. Artists from all over the world visit Williamsburg to leave their imprint on the city's walls, resulting in an ever-changing outdoor exhibition. The streets of the area are like an open-air museum where visitors may explore and enjoy these artists' ingenuity and talent.

Venues for Music

Williamsburg has a robust music scene with a variety of venues catering to various musical interests. The Music Hall of Williamsburg is a well-known venue that produces concerts by both local and international acts from a variety of genres. Another prominent music venue is Brooklyn Steel, which is noted for its cutting-edge amenities and an excellent list of artists. These establishments add to the neighborhood's reputation as a live music magnet.

Theater

Theatergoers will have much to do in Williamsburg as well. The Brick Theatre is a well-known performance venue that features experimental theatrical works by new playwrights. Its tiny environment and diversified programming provide a one-of-a-kind theater experience for both artists and audiences. Furthermore, the Williamsburg Theatre Festival features a diverse spectrum of theatrical events, including plays, musicals, and immersive experiences.

Cultural Happenings

Throughout the year, Williamsburg presents a range of cultural events that showcase the neighborhood's artistic culture. The Northside Festival is a three-day festival that includes live music, film screenings, art exhibits, and technology conferences. It invites artists, singers, filmmakers, and entrepreneurs together to present their work and stimulate innovation. Another notable event that encourages independent cinema and exhibits a varied range of films from around the world is the Bushwick Film Festival.

Cafes and Taverns

The arts and culture scene in Williamsburg is not restricted to galleries and performing venues. The area is also recognized for its thriving café and bar scene, where artists and creatives frequently congregate to socialize and collaborate. There are numerous locations to relax and absorb the artistic ambiance while enjoying a drink or a meal, ranging from quaint coffee shops to contemporary cocktail clubs.

Artists from the area

Williamsburg has a strong community of local craftsmen who create one-of-a-kind handmade things. From jewelry makers to ceramic artists, these entrepreneurs contribute to the creative landscape of the neighborhood. Visitors can browse local markets and stores to find one-of-a-kind things that reflect Williamsburg's artistic culture.

Brighton Beach and Coney Island

Coney Island and Brighton Beach in Brooklyn are two prominent destinations that provide visitors with a distinct and vivid experience. These communities in southern Brooklyn are known for their rich history, diversified culture, and intriguing attractions. Coney Island and Brighton Beach offer it all: thrilling rides, sandy beaches, delectable food, and cultural activities.

Coney Island, New York

Coney Island is a peninsula in the Atlantic Ocean known for its amusement parks, boardwalk, and vibrant atmosphere. Since the late 1800s, it has been a favorite site for both New Yorkers and tourists. Several amusement parks are located in the region, including Luna Park, which boasts thrilling rides such as the Cyclone roller coaster and the Wonder Wheel. The New York Aquarium is another noteworthy site, where tourists can explore numerous marine displays.

Aside from its entertainment parks, Coney Island is famous for its iconic boardwalk. The boardwalk, which stretches for approximately 2.7 miles down the oceanfront, provides spectacular views of the ocean and is lined with food booths, stores, and entertainment venues. Visitors can indulge in classic carnival foods like Nathan's Famous hot dogs or a range of ethnic cuisines available in the vicinity.

Throughout the summer, Coney Island organizes a variety of events and festivals that draw visitors from all over the world. The Mermaid Parade, which features colorful costumes, floats, and live entertainment, is one of the most popular annual events. Fireworks displays, concerts, and sand sculpting competitions are among the other festivities.

Brighton Pier

Brighton Beach, located immediately east of Coney Island, is known as "Little Odesa" because of its significant concentration of Russian-speaking immigrants from Ukraine and Russia. With its Russian stores, restaurants, and community centers, this dynamic neighborhood provides a one-of-a-kind cultural experience.

Brighton Beach's lovely sandy beach is one of its key draws. Visitors can unwind on the beach, swim in the ocean, or stroll along the promenade. Volleyball courts, playgrounds, and picnic spots are also available for use by families and friends at the beach.

Brighton Beach Avenue, the neighborhood's principal commercial street, is lined with Russian markets, bakeries, and restaurants. Visitors can sample a wide variety of Russian food, including traditional dishes such as borscht, pelmeni, and blini. The neighborhood is also known for its vibrant nightlife, with various bars and clubs open till the early hours of the morning.

Brighton Beach has various cultural facilities for anyone interested in learning about Russian culture and history. The Brighton Beach Library has a substantial collection of Russian literature and hosts book readings and seminars. Throughout the year, the Russian American Foundation conducts a variety of cultural events, including art exhibitions, music concerts, and film screenings.

Museums and historical sites

Brooklyn, one of New York City's five boroughs, is a treasure trove of history and culture. Brooklyn, with its rich tradition and diverse population, has a plethora of historic buildings and museums that provide visitors with an insight into its past. A complete reference to Brooklyn's historic buildings and institutions, from prominent landmarks to lesser-known jewels.

1. The Brooklyn Museum

The Brooklyn Museum, located in the center of Prospect Park, is one of the country's largest art museums. It was founded in 1895 and houses a large collection of ancient Egyptian artifacts,

American art, European artwork, African art, and other items. In addition, the museum features rotating exhibitions that feature modern artists and thought-provoking installations.

2. New York Historical Society

The Brooklyn Historical Society is dedicated to preserving and promoting Brooklyn's history. The society, which is housed in a lovely historic building in Brooklyn Heights, provides exhibitions, educational events, and research resources for individuals interested in learning about the borough's history. Photographs, maps, documents, and oral histories in the society's collection provide valuable insights into Brooklyn's evolution.

3. The Green-Wood Cemetery

Green-Wood Cemetery is a living memorial to Brooklyn's history as well as a final resting place. This National Historic Landmark, which was established in 1838, spans over 478 acres and is home to gorgeous architecture, exquisite mausoleums, and beautiful landscapes. Many renowned New Yorkers, including artists, politicians, and innovators, are buried here. Visitors can take guided tours to learn about the cemetery's significance or simply meander through its grounds on their own.

4. Wyckoff Farmhouse Museum is located in Wyckoff, New Jersey

The Wyckoff Farmhouse Museum, which dates back to 1652, transports you back in time. This historic mansion in Brooklyn's Flatbush area provides a look into colonial life. Visitors can walk through the completely furnished chambers and learn about the daily lives of the Wyckoff family, who were among the area's first Dutch inhabitants. In addition, the museum hosts programs and workshops that explore various areas of early American history.

5. New York Transit Museum (NYTM)

The New York Transit Museum, housed in a former subway station in Downtown Brooklyn, is a must-see for transportation lovers and history buffs alike. The museum depicts the evolution of New York City public transportation with vintage subway vehicles, buses, and interactive exhibits. Visitors can tour the underground platforms, learn about the city's famed metro system, and even operate an ancient bus.

6. Heritage Center of Weeksville

Weeksville Heritage Center is an undiscovered treasure that tells the narrative of one of America's earliest free Black towns. Weeksville, founded in 1838, was a shelter for African Americans during a time of slavery and bigotry. The cultural center preserves four ancient houses that were previously part of this village, and it offers guided tours, exhibitions, and educational events that shed light on the area's rich past.

7. Museum at Coney Island

Coney Island is well-known for its amusement parks and beachfront, but it also includes a museum committed to preserving its lively history. The Coney Island Museum displays antiques, pictures, and memorabilia from the area's heyday as an amusement park. Visitors may immerse themselves in the nostalgia of this cherished site by learning about the history of iconic attractions such as the Cyclone roller coaster and the Wonder Wheel.

8. The Aged Stone House

The Old Stone House is a rebuilt 17th-century Dutch farmhouse that played an important role in the American Revolutionary War battle of Brooklyn. This historic property, located in Park Slope's Washington Park, offers exhibitions, educational activities, and community events that emphasize its historical significance. Visitors can explore the house's period chambers, examine the Battle of Brooklyn artifacts, and relax in the neighboring park.

9. Historic Lefferts House

The Lefferts Historic House, located in Prospect Park, is a living museum that transports visitors to the 18th century. This Dutch Colonial farmhouse, built in 1783, depicts the lifestyle and traditions of early Brooklyn residents. Visitors can learn about Brooklyn's history by participating in hands-on activities, watching demonstrations of old crafts, and exploring the house's period rooms.

10. Museum on the Waterfront

The Waterfront Museum, housed in a historic barge anchored in Red Hook, provides a unique viewpoint on Brooklyn's nautical legacy. Exhibits in the museum cover the history of New York City's waterfront, including its industrial background and the importance of barges in the transportation of products. Visitors can tour the interior of the barge, learn about nautical customs, and even attend live performances and activities on its deck.

Chapter 3: Culinary Delights

Brooklyn's Diverse Food Scene

Brooklyn, one of the five boroughs of New York City, is known for its bustling and diversified food culture. With its rich cultural background and a melting pot of communities, the borough provides a variety of gastronomic pleasures to suit all palates. Brooklyn has something for everyone, from classic ethnic cuisines to modern fusion restaurants. Let's take a look at the various aspects of Brooklyn's diversified food scene.

1. Ethnic Traditional Cuisines

Brooklyn is home to a diverse range of ethnic cultures, each with its culinary traditions. There are authentic meals from Italy, China, Mexico, India, Greece, and many more nations. Exploring Brooklyn's different neighborhoods invites you to embark on a worldwide gastronomic tour, from substantial Italian pasta dishes in Bensonhurst to delectable dumplings in Sunset Park's Chinatown.

2. Fusion Restaurants That Are Trendy

Brooklyn also embraces the fusion food trend, in which chefs combine many culinary traditions to produce unique and entertaining dishes. By integrating products and techniques from diverse cultures, these eateries put a fresh spin on classic meals. Whether it's Korean-Mexican tacos or Japanese-Italian fusion sushi rolls, Brooklyn has a plethora of interesting and excellent fusion options.

3. Farm-to-Table Revolution

Brooklyn has enthusiastically embraced the farm-to-table trend. Many of the borough's restaurants prioritize using locally produced products from nearby farms and sources. This commitment to fresh and sustainable products guarantees that guests can enjoy the flavors of seasonal delicacies while supporting local farmers and lowering carbon footprints.

4. Markets and Food Halls

Brooklyn has various food halls and markets that offer a diverse range of gastronomic options under one roof. These dynamic areas bring together a variety of merchants serving various cuisines, allowing guests to enjoy a variety of flavors in a single visit. From Smorgasburg in Williamsburg, which has a variety of food booths and exhibitors, to the busy Brooklyn Flea Market, which has an eclectic mix of culinary options, these foodie hotspots are a must-see for any foodie.

5. Iconic Brooklyn Cuisine

No trip to Brooklyn's food scene would be complete without mentioning its most famous meals. The neighborhood is well-known for its iconic New York-style pizza, with places like Di Fara Pizza in Midwood and Grimaldi's in DUMBO attracting pizza fans from all around. Furthermore, Brooklyn is well-known for its bagels, with establishments such as Bagel Hole in Park Slope and Tompkins Square Bagels in Williamsburg serving up scrumptious masterpieces. The egg cream, a delightful beverage prepared with chocolate syrup, milk, and seltzer, and the black-and-white cookie, soft vanilla, and chocolate frosted confection, are two more renowned Brooklyn delicacies.

Cafés and bakeries that are trendy

Brooklyn is recognized for its robust food culture, which includes trendy cafés and bakeries. Whether you like coffee or have a sweet appetite, Brooklyn has plenty of places to satiate your tastes. From quiet neighborhood hangouts to hipster hangouts, here are some of Brooklyn's finest trendy cafés and bakeries:

Sweatshop

Sweatshop, located in Williamsburg, is a renowned café noted for its great coffee and relaxed atmosphere. They acquire their beans from local roasters and provide a variety of brewing methods to accommodate a variety of preferences. The café also provides delectable pastries and small meals, making it ideal for breakfast or brunch.

Maman

Maman, which has many locations around Brooklyn, is a delightful café that combines French flare with local food. Their menu includes traditional French pastries such as croissants and pain au chocolat, as well as savory items such as quiches and sandwiches. Maman is a must-visit for breakfast or afternoon tea because of its intimate setting and courteous personnel.

Five Branches

Five Leaves, located in Greenpoint, is not only a café but also a popular neighborhood gathering.

Five Leaves is known for its Australian-inspired cuisine, which includes a large selection of coffee drinks as well as delectable brunch items such as ricotta pancakes and avocado toast. The rustic design and outdoor seating area of the café contribute to its allure.

Bakery

Bakeri, located in the center of Williamsburg, is a charming bakery that emanates charm and friendliness. Their freshly baked bread, pastries, and cakes are crafted using premium ingredients, resulting in exquisite delicacies that keep customers returning for more. Bakeri also has a comfortable seating area where you may enjoy your baked goodies while sipping a cup of coffee or tea.

Scotch and butter

Butter & Scotch in Crown Heights is a must-see for those with a sweet craving. This bakery specializes in boozy delicacies and exotic cocktails, such as bourbon ginger pecan pie and whiskey caramel cake. Butter & Scotch is a notable destination for indulgence thanks to its lively ambiance, courteous service, and unique menu.

These are just a few of the fashionable cafés and bakeries available in Brooklyn. Exploring the borough's food scene is an adventure in and of itself, whether you're a local or a guest. So, the next time you're in Brooklyn, check out these places and find your new favorite place for coffee or pastries.

Famous Brooklyn Pizzerias

Brooklyn, New York is known for its bustling food scene, and one of the borough's most recognizable and adored culinary offerings is pizza. Brooklyn's pizzerias have become famous attractions for both locals and visitors, thanks to their rich history and varied range of styles. From traditional Neapolitan pizzas to avant-garde innovations, here are 10 of the most iconic Brooklyn pizzerias you must visit.

Pizza Di Fara

Di Fara Pizza, located in Brooklyn's Midwood district, is widely regarded as one of the best pizzerias in the entire city. Domenico DeMarco founded this family-owned institution in 1964, and it has earned a cult following for its precisely prepared pizzas. Every pie is carefully overseen by DeMarco, who hand-stretches the dough, adds fresh ingredients, and bakes it to perfection in a coal-fired oven. As a result, the thin-crust pizza has a great flavor balance that keeps people coming back for more.

Pizzeria Grimaldi

Grimaldi's Pizzeria, located under the Brooklyn Bridge in DUMBO (Down Under the Manhattan Bridge Overpass), is another legendary landmark with global notoriety. This pizza has been in operation since 1905 when it was known as Patsy's Pizza. Grimaldi's coal-fired brick oven produces a distinctively charred and crispy crust that complements their fresh toppings and handmade sauce. The vintage décor and vistas of the Manhattan skyline enhance the overall eating experience at this Brooklyn landmark.

Lucali

Lucali, tucked away in Carroll Gardens, is a quaint and intimate pizzeria known for serving some of Brooklyn's greatest wood-fired pizzas. There are only two options on the menu: a typical margarita pizza and a white pizza topped with garlic, mozzarella, and ricotta. The dough is produced daily in-house, and the toppings are purchased from local markets to ensure the most flavorful results. Lucali provides an amazing dining experience with its candlelight environment and BYOB policy.

Totonno's Napolitano Pizzeria

Totonno's Pizzeria Napolitano in Coney Island is one of Brooklyn's oldest pizzerias, having opened in 1924. For centuries, this family-owned restaurant has served outstanding thin-crust pizzas. Totonno's is noted for its no-frills approach to pizza, employing only the finest ingredients and a coal-fired oven to produce the perfect balance of tastes. The original Margherita pizza is a must-order here, exemplifying the simplicity and excellence that have made Totonno's a long-standing favorite.

Roberta's

Roberta's, located in the trendy Bushwick district, is not only a pizzeria but also a gourmet destination in its own right. Roberta's has received significant accolades for its inventive and innovative approach to pizza when it first opened its doors in 2008. Their wood-fired pies are made with fresh ingredients from their on-site garden and surrounding farmers. The restaurant itself emits a hip and laid-back attitude, making it a popular destination for residents and travelers seeking a great dining experience.

These legendary Brooklyn pizzerias exemplify the borough's pizza scene's diversity and excellence. Whether you want a typical Neapolitan pie or something a little more daring, these restaurants have a variety of selections that will satisfy any pizza fan.

Street Food and Markets

Brooklyn, one of New York City's five boroughs, is recognized for its dynamic food culture and various culinary choices. The neighborhood is home to several food markets and street food sellers that highlight the city's multicultural flavors and cuisines. From artisanal food markets to bustling street food festivals, Brooklyn's food markets and street food scene provide a diverse selection of delectable options for both locals and visitors.

1. Smorgasburg

Smorgasburg is one of Brooklyn's most prominent food markets. During the summer, it takes place every weekend at various places throughout the borough, including Williamsburg and Prospect Park. Smorgasburg, with over 100 food vendors, offers a broad array of foods ranging from international street food to regional delicacies. Visitors can savor delectable foods including lobster rolls, ramen burgers, premium ice cream, and much more.

2. The Brooklyn Flea

Another well-known market that mixes vintage discoveries with exquisite food offers is Brooklyn Flea. This market has a diverse selection of antique sellers, crafters, and food vendors. Visitors can browse the unusual stalls selling vintage clothing, jewelry, and furniture before stopping for a bite to eat at one of the many food sellers. Brooklyn Flea has something for everyone, from wood-fired pizza to gourmet sandwiches and handcrafted pastries.

3. Square Smorg

Smorg Square, located in Downtown Brooklyn, is a year-round outdoor market that features some of the greatest local food vendors in the neighborhood. In comparison to Smorgasburg, it has a more permanent arrangement, with a variety of stalls providing anything from Mexican street tacos to Korean BBQ and vegan delights. There is also a beer garden where tourists can unwind and enjoy their meals.

4. Market Hall in Dekalb

Dekalb Market Hall is a Downtown Brooklyn indoor food hall. It is home to over 40 food vendors, ranging from well-known eateries to new culinary concepts. Visitors can sample traditional New York-style deli sandwiches, gourmet pizza, soul cuisine, Chinese dumplings, and other dishes. Dekalb Market Hall is ideal for people wishing to enjoy a variety of cuisines under one roof.

5. Red Hook Restaurants

The Red Hook Food Vendors in Brooklyn are a must-see for a genuine street food experience. This outdoor market brings together a variety of Latin American food vendors who provide delicious and reasonably priced fare. Visitors may taste the delicacies of Mexico, El Salvador, Colombia, and more, from tacos and pupusas to ceviche and empanadas. Red Hook Food

Vendors has become a neighborhood institution, attracting foodies from all over the city.

Distilleries and Craft Breweries

Brooklyn, New York has become a center for craft breweries and distilleries, providing visitors with a broad and unique drinking experience. The borough, which has a long history of brewing and distilling, is home to a diverse range of establishments that manufacture high-quality craft beers and spirits. Brooklyn's craft brewers and distilleries have something for everyone, whether you're a beer enthusiast or a whiskey connoisseur.

Brooklyn Craft Breweries

Brooklyn Brewing Company

Brooklyn Brewery, founded in 1988, is a forerunner in the American craft beer movement. Their taproom in Williamsburg serves a broad variety of beers, including their signature Brooklyn Lager and famous seasonal brews. Visitors can take guided tours of the brewery and enjoy tastings while learning about the brewing process.

Threes Brewing Company

Threes Brewing, located in Gowanus, is noted for its unique and experimental approach to brewing. On tap, they provide a rotating assortment of beers ranging from classic styles to interesting collaborations with other breweries. The large taproom also holds events such as live music and pop-up food vendors.

The Other Half Is Brewing

Other Half Brewing, located in Carroll Gardens, is known for its hop-forward beers. They are known for their juicy IPAs and double IPAs, which have a cult following among beer fans. The taproom has an industrial-chic vibe and frequently organizes can releases where visitors can buy limited-edition brews.

Artisanal Ales by Grimm

Grimm Artisanal Ales, founded by a husband-and-wife duo, specializes in small-batch, flavor-driven brews. Their East Williamsburg taproom features an ever-changing range of beers that demonstrate their devotion to quality and originality. Visitors can partake in tasting flights or purchase cans to go.

Brewing Transmitter

Transmitter Brewing, located in Long Island City, just across the East River from Brooklyn, specializes in farmhouse-style ales and sour brews. To achieve unique and complex flavors, they use traditional brewing processes and local ingredients. Visitors can enjoy their beers in a friendly ambiance in the intimate tavern.

Brooklyn distilleries

Distillery in Kings County

Kings County Distillery, New York City's oldest operational whiskey distillery, has acquired recognition for its handcrafted spirits. They make small-batch whiskeys, bourbon, moonshine, and other spirits at the Brooklyn Navy Yard using ancient distilling procedures. Visitors to the distillery can enjoy guided tours and try their award-winning products.

The New York Distillery Company

The New York Distilling Company, located in Williamsburg, is well-known for its gin manufacture. They make a variety of gins, including their flagship Dorothy Parker American Gin, which is named after the famous writer and poet. The distillery also provides tours where guests may learn about the gin-making process and sample the finished product.

Distillery in Industry City

Industry City Distillery, located in Sunset Park, specializes in creating vodka using environmentally friendly methods. To create their smooth and tasty vodka, they use locally obtained ingredients and a unique fermentation procedure. Visitors can try their spirits and learn about their environmentally friendly approach at their tasting room.

Still House, Van Brunt

Van Brunt Stillhouse, founded by a former architect, makes small-batch whiskey, rum, and other spirits in Red Hook. They employ locally grown grains and traditional distilling ways to create their unique goods. The distillery gives tours that give guests an insight into their production process and allow them to sample their spirits.

The Brooklyn Gin

Brooklyn Gin is known for its artisanal approach to gin-making, producing handcrafted gins steeped with botanicals imported from all over the world. Their Brooklyn Navy Yard distillery offers tours where visitors may learn about the distillation process and try their distinctive gin blends.

Visiting Brooklyn's craft breweries and distilleries allows you to learn about the city's thriving beer and spirits culture. There are lots of options to suit your taste buds, whether you want to try traditional styles or creative brews. Each location, from major brewers like Brooklyn Brewery to smaller, inventive operations like Threes Brewing, provides a unique experience for tourists. Similarly, Brooklyn distilleries such as Kings County Distillery and New York Distilling Company exhibit the artistry and expertise that goes into making spirits.

Overall, Brooklyn's artisan breweries and distilleries add to the borough's vibrant culinary scene, attracting both locals and tourists. Exploring these enterprises allows guests to immerse themselves in Brooklyn's rich brewing and distilling traditions while sampling a variety of flavors and styles.

Chapter 4: Local Experiences

Brooklyn's Arts and Music Scene

Brooklyn, one of New York City's five boroughs, is known for its thriving arts and music scene. The borough is home to a wide group of artists, musicians, and creative people, making it a cultural hotspot. Brooklyn has a plethora of options for art and music fans, ranging from world-class art galleries to underground music venues. This is a thorough guide to the arts and music scene in Brooklyn.

Galleries of Art

Brooklyn is home to a plethora of art galleries that present a diverse range of artistic styles and mediums. The Brooklyn Museum is a well-known art venue in the borough. The Prospect Heights Museum of Art includes a large collection of art from numerous periods and civilizations. It includes works by well-known artists such as Frida Kahlo, Georgia O'Keeffe, and Andy Warhol.

The MoMA PS1 is another prominent art gallery in Brooklyn. This modern art institution, located in Long Island City, just across the East River from Brooklyn, showcases cutting-edge works by rising artists. Regular activities at the gallery include performances, film screenings, and conversations.

Williamsburg is a must-see neighborhood for visitors interested in discovering the local art scene. Williamsburg, known for its thriving street art scene, is home to numerous tiny galleries that feature works by local artists. The Boiler, Pierogi Gallery, and Front Room Gallery are among of the area's most popular galleries.

Venues for Music

The music scene in Brooklyn is similarly broad and active. The borough has a long history of supporting a wide range of musical genres, from indie rock to hip-hop and jazz. The Barclays Center is a well-known concert venue in Brooklyn. This cutting-edge venue in Downtown Brooklyn hosts significant events by internationally known musicians.

The Brooklyn Steel is another noteworthy music venue. This huge warehouse-turned-concert space in East Williamsburg has quickly become a favorite among both local and visiting bands. Brooklyn Steel provides an amazing live music experience thanks to its exceptional acoustics and capacity to handle big audiences.

Baby's All Right in Williamsburg and Union Pool in Greenpoint are popular choices for people looking for a more intimate atmosphere. These smaller venues include a combination of live music performances, DJ sets, and special events to highlight rising artists.

Public Art

Many excellent graffiti artists use Brooklyn's streets as a canvas. The borough's strong street art movement provides color and character to its neighborhoods, from large-scale murals to delicate graffiti tags. Bushwick, in particular, has a strong street art culture. The walls and buildings of the area are covered with amazing artworks by both local and foreign artists.

A guided tour is one of the greatest ways to discover Brooklyn's street art. Several firms provide walking or biking tours of the borough's most active street art sites. These tours provide visitors with an understanding of the artists' histories, skills, and the stories behind their paintings.

Festivals and Special Events

Throughout the year, Brooklyn organizes a plethora of festivals and events that celebrate the arts and music. The Brooklyn Museum's First Saturday is one of the most well-known events. Every first Saturday of the month, the museum opens its doors for free and hosts an evening of live performances, art-making workshops, film screenings, and other activities.

The Northside Festival, hosted in Williamsburg and Greenpoint, is another noteworthy festival. This multi-day festival features a wide range of musical performances, film screenings, art exhibitions, and technology conferences. It gives established and young artists a place to showcase their talents.

Additionally, as part of its Celebrate Brooklyn! program, Prospect Park holds several outdoor performances during the summer. Festival. This free concert series showcases a combination of local and globally famous musicians performing outdoors.

Shopping at Distinctive Boutiques

Brooklyn is well-known for its dynamic and diversified shopping environment, which features a wide range of distinctive boutiques catering to all interests and styles. This lively district has something for everyone, from fashionable fashion boutiques to vintage shops and specialty retailers. Whether you're a fashionista looking for the latest trends or a vintage enthusiast looking for one-of-a-kind treasures, Brooklyn's shopping culture offers it all. In this complete travel guide, we'll look at some of Brooklyn's top districts and stores for a memorable shopping trip.

1. Williamsburg

Williamsburg, one of Brooklyn's most popular neighborhoods, is a refuge for fashionable stores and independent designers. Bedford Avenue, Williamsburg's main avenue, is lined with an astounding array of businesses selling one-of-a-kind clothes, accessories, and home items. Bird, a high-end women's boutique known for its carefully curated selection of designer pieces, Catbird, a jewelry store known for its delicate and minimalist designs, and Beacon's Closet, a beloved vintage shop where you can find hidden gems at affordable prices, are just a few of the notable boutiques in Williamsburg.

2. DUMBO

DUMBO (Down Under the Manhattan Bridge Overpass), located between the Manhattan and Brooklyn Bridges, has grown as a fashionable neighborhood with a bustling arts scene and an outstanding assortment of stores. DUMBO's main shopping districts, Main Street and Front Street, provide a mix of well-known brands and local designers. Powerhouse Arena is a must-see bookstore that presents literary events and exhibitions regularly. Journey Home offers an eclectic mix of furniture, fabrics, and accessories collected from around the world for unique home decor goods. Modern Anthology, which focuses on men's clothing and grooming goods, and Trunk Vintage & Handmade, which sells vintage clothing and handmade accessories, are two more famous DUMBO businesses.

3. The Park Slope

Park Slope, known for its lush lanes and gorgeous brownstone residences, is a pleasant neighborhood with a strong shopping environment. Fifth Avenue is Park Slope's primary shopping street, lined with boutiques, specialized stores, and local companies. Thistle & Clover, a store that focuses on sustainable and ethically created products, has fashionable clothes and accessories. Stop by Homebody Boutique for one-of-a-kind gifts and home decor products. It features a carefully curated range of handmade goods from local craftsmen. Bird Brooklyn, a sister store to the Williamsburg location, and Olive & Bette's, a women's clothing store recognized for its trendy and stylish products, are two more famous Park Slope boutiques.

4. Cobblestone Hill

Cobble Hill, located between Brooklyn Heights and Carroll Gardens, is a lovely neighborhood with a small-town feel. Court route is Cobble Hill's major shopping route, with a variety of stores, restaurants, and cafes. Visit Article&, a shop that features emerging designers from around the world, for fashion-forward clothing and accessories. Catbird's original location in Cobble Hill is a must-see for unusual jewelry pieces. By Brooklyn, which features a wide range of locally manufactured products, and Staubitz Market, an old-school butcher store that has been serving the community since 1917, are two other famous boutiques in Cobble Hill.

5. Fort Greene, New York

Fort Greene is a bustling area with a thriving shopping scene located near the cultural core of

BAM (Brooklyn Academy of Music). Fulton route is Fort Greene's major retail route, with an eclectic mix of boutiques and specialty stores. Visit Stuart & Wright, a boutique recognized for its carefully curated assortment of designer products, for one-of-a-kind clothes and accessories for men and women. Beacon's Closet has another store in Fort Greene for vintage fans to peruse through shelves of secondhand clothing and accessories. Other famous Fort Greene businesses include The Green Grape, a gourmet food store that also sells artisanal wines and spirits, and Greenlight Bookstore, an independent bookstore that conducts author events and readings regularly.

Parks and Outdoor Recreation

Brooklyn, one of New York City's five boroughs, is recognized for its vibrant culture, diversified neighborhoods, and beautiful parks and outdoor activities. With over 30 parks located across the borough, Brooklyn provides a diverse range of recreational possibilities for both residents and visitors. This lively urban sanctuary has something for everyone, from huge green spaces to seaside parks.

1. Prospect Park (NY)

Prospect Park is one of Brooklyn's most recognizable parks. Prospect Park spans over 500 acres and was designed by Frederick Law Olmsted and Calvert Vaux, the same architects who designed Manhattan's Central Park. The park has winding routes for walking and jogging, large meadows for picnics or sunbathing, and several playgrounds for kids. Long Meadow, a huge open region within the park, is perfect for sports like soccer and frisbee. Visitors can also rent a paddleboat to explore the park's lake or relax at the Prospect Park Zoo, which is located inside its boundaries.

2. Park on the Brooklyn Bridge

Brooklyn Bridge Park, located along the East River and offering stunning views of the Manhattan skyline, has become a popular destination for both locals and tourists. This 1.3-mile-long beachfront park provides a variety of recreational opportunities. Visitors can stroll or cycle down the promenade, eat on the verdant lawns, or play beach volleyball on the sand courts. The park also has various piers where people can go fishing or simply relax and enjoy the scenery. Basketball courts, soccer fields, and playgrounds are also available for sports fans of all ages.

3. Marine Reserve

Marine Park, located in southeastern Brooklyn, is one of the borough's largest parks. Its 800-acre size allows for plenty of area for outdoor activities including hiking, bird-watching, and picnicking. The Salt Marsh Nature Center is located in the park and offers educational events and exhibits on the local fauna and habitat. Visitors can also enjoy boating and fishing at the park's freshwater kayak launch, as well as a stroll along the park's gorgeous waterfront.

4. Park McCarren

McCarren Park, located in the stylish Williamsburg area, is a thriving hub for outdoor activities. This 35-acre park has a huge open field that is ideal for sports such as soccer, baseball, and ultimate frisbee. There is also a swimming pool, tennis courts, and a running track in the park. McCarren Park provides outdoor concerts and movie screenings in the summer, attracting both locals and visitors. Furthermore, the park is bordered by a plethora of cafes, restaurants, and stores, making it a great place for a day of outdoor fun followed by an exploration of the dynamic surrounding environment.

5. Greenwood Memorial Park

Greenwood Cemetery, while not your usual park, provides a unique outdoor experience in Brooklyn. This historic cemetery, which spans 478 acres, is known for its exquisite landscape architecture and serves as the final resting place for many prominent personalities. Visitors can walk around the cemetery's winding walks, see its gorgeous monuments and mausoleums, and take guided tours to learn about its rich history. Greenwood Cemetery also hosts events such as concerts and outdoor yoga courses, making it a tranquil place to relax.

Aside from these prominent parks, Brooklyn is densely packed with smaller green areas and pocket parks that provide a reprieve from the city's hectic streets. Fort Greene Park, Sunset Park, Owl's Head Park, and Highland Park are just a few examples. Each park has its distinct personality and amenities, giving tourists lots of alternatives when looking for outdoor activities in Brooklyn.

Entertainment and Nightlife

The nightlife and entertainment scene in Brooklyn is bustling, diversified, and ever-changing. After the sun goes down, this New York City borough has something for everyone, from trendy pubs to live music venues. Exploring Brooklyn's nightlife, whether you're a local or a visitor, can be an exciting and unforgettable experience. We will delve into the numerous parts of Brooklyn's nightlife and entertainment in this complete travel guide, including prominent neighborhoods, bars, clubs, music venues, theaters, and cultural events.

Neighborhoods

Brooklyn is divided into several areas, each with its own distinct nightlife and leisure opportunities. Williamsburg, Greenpoint, Bushwick, DUMBO (Down Under the Manhattan Bridge Overpass), Park Slope, Gowanus, and Red Hook are among the most popular nightlife neighborhoods in Brooklyn.

Bars

Brooklyn has a diverse range of bars to suit all interests and inclinations. This borough has plenty of options for you, whether you're looking for a quaint local pub or a fashionable cocktail bar. The Four Horsemen in Williamsburg, Maison Premiere in Greenpoint, The Narrows in Bushwick, Bar Tabac in Cobble Hill, and The Clover Club in Carroll Gardens are just a few of the prominent bars in Brooklyn.

Clubs

Brooklyn offers a vibrant club culture for individuals who prefer dancing the night away to throbbing sounds and energetic DJ sets. Clubs are catering to diverse electronic music genres and interests, ranging from subterranean techno clubs to upscale dance venues. Output in Williamsburg, Good Room in Greenpoint, Nowadays in Ridgewood (near the Brooklyn border), House of Yes in Bushwick, and Elsewhere in East Williamsburg are all popular clubs in Brooklyn.

Venues for Music

Brooklyn has long been known as a live music hub. Numerous music venues dot the landscape of the borough, providing platforms for both established and developing musicians of all genres. Brooklyn Steel in East Williamsburg, Music Hall of Williamsburg in Williamsburg, Rough Trade NYC in Williamsburg, Baby's All Right in Williamsburg, and Union Pool in Williamsburg are some renowned music venues in Brooklyn.

Theaters

Brooklyn is home to several theaters that present a diverse spectrum of acts such as plays, musicals, comedy shows, and more. These theaters provide cultural experiences as well as entertainment options for theatergoers. The Brooklyn Academy of Music (BAM) in Fort Greene, Kings Theatre in Flatbush, St. Ann's Warehouse in DUMBO, BRIC Arts Media

House in Fort Greene, and The Brick Theater in Williamsburg are all notable theaters in Brooklyn.

Cultural Happenings

Throughout the year, Brooklyn presents a variety of cultural events that allow residents and visitors to explore art, music, cinema, gastronomy, and other topics. The Brooklyn Hip-Hop Festival, Northside Festival in Williamsburg and Greenpoint, the Coney Island Mermaid Parade, and Celebrate Brooklyn! are all popular cultural events. The Brooklyn Book Festival and the Summer Concert Series at Prospect Park Bandshell.

The nightlife and entertainment scene in Brooklyn is continuously changing, with new pubs, clubs, music venues, theaters, and cultural events opening regularly. Exploring the thriving nightlife of this borough can be a fascinating excursion for anyone looking for memorable experiences after dark.

Festivals and Events in the Community

Brooklyn, one of New York City's five boroughs, is a thriving and varied neighborhood that hosts a variety of community events and festivals throughout the year. These events highlight the borough's rich culture, history, and traditions, attracting both locals and visitors. There is always something spectacular going on in Brooklyn, from music festivals to food fairs.

The Brooklyn Hip-Hop Festival is one of the most popular community events in Brooklyn. This festival, held each July, honors the iconic genre of hip-hop through live performances by renowned artists, seminars, panel discussions, film screenings, and more. It serves as a showcase for budding talent while also paying homage to hip-hop's forefathers.

The Coney Island Mermaid Parade is another noteworthy event in Brooklyn. This whimsical and colorful procession, held in June, features participants dressed as mermaids, mermen, and other sea animals. It is a celebration of art, innovation, and the distinct Coney Island attitude. Thousands of onlookers throng the streets to catch a peek at the exotic costumes and enjoy the colorful atmosphere of the procession.

The Taste of Bushwick festival is a must-attend event for foodies. This annual gastronomic feast highlights Bushwick's unique culinary culture, one of Brooklyn's trendiest districts. Local restaurants and food sellers provide samples of their specialty dishes, allowing guests to enjoy a wide range of flavors and cuisines. The celebratory atmosphere is enhanced by live music performances and art installations.

Celebrate Brooklyn! may be seen in Prospect Park. festival. This summer-long series of concerts and shows at Prospect Park Bandshell draws music fans from all over the city. The schedule features a combination of local and globally acclaimed musicians from jazz, rock, indie, world music, and other genres. Attendees are encouraged to bring blankets or chairs to enjoy the shows beneath the stars.

The West Indian American Day Carnival is also a lively celebration of Caribbean culture and heritage. This carnival, held on Labor Day in the Crown Heights neighborhood, boasts colorful costumes, boisterous music, dance acts, and delectable Caribbean cuisine. The grand parade, in which people march through the streets dressed in elaborate costumes representing various Caribbean countries, is the event's climax.

These are just a few of the many community activities and festivals held in Brooklyn throughout the year. The diversified population and rich cultural legacy of the borough contribute to a vibrant calendar of events that cater to a wide range of interests and tastes. There is always an event or festival waiting to be discovered, whether you are a music lover, foodie, art enthusiast, or simply looking to immerse yourself in the colorful environment of Brooklyn.

Chapter 5: Practical Information

Accommodation Options

Brooklyn, one of New York City's five boroughs, has a diverse range of lodging alternatives for visitors. Brooklyn provides something to satisfy any traveler's wants and interests, whether they like luxurious hotels, budget-friendly hostels, or pleasant bed and breakfasts. Staying in Brooklyn might be a terrific decision for your vacation to New York City, thanks to its bustling neighborhoods, diversified culture, and easy access to Manhattan.

Hotels

Brooklyn is home to several high-end hotels that offer luxurious lodgings and first-rate services. These hotels frequently have big rooms with contemporary decor, on-site restaurants and bars, fitness centers, and concierge services. The William Vale, 1 Hotel Brooklyn Bridge, and The Hoxton are among the most popular luxury hotels in Brooklyn.

There are various mid-range and budget-friendly hotels in Brooklyn for tourists on a restricted budget. These hotels provide pleasant rooms at lower prices without sacrificing quality. The Box House Hotel, Hotel Le Bleu, and The Tillary Hotel are other notable mid-range options.

Hostels

If you want to travel on a budget or prefer the social environment of hostels, Brooklyn provides various possibilities for you. Hostels offer shared dormitory-style lodging with communal areas for visitors to meet and socialize. They are ideal for lone travelers or those wishing to meet other adventures. The Local NYC, NY Moore Hostel, and International Students Residence are among the notable Brooklyn hostels.

Bed and breakfast establishments

Consider staying at one of Brooklyn's beautiful bed & breakfasts for a more intimate and homey experience. These places usually have individually furnished rooms, customized service, and prepared breakfasts. Akwaaba

Mansion Bed & Breakfast, Lefferts Manor Bed & Breakfast, and Sankofa Aban Bed & Breakfast are among the most popular bed and breakfasts in Brooklyn.

Airbnb

Airbnb is another popular option for Brooklyn lodging. Airbnb offers a more local and immersive experience for guests, with listings ranging from private rooms to entire flats or houses. It enables guests to stay in distinct areas and engage with locals, giving them a flavor of the authentic Brooklyn lifestyle.

Rentals for a limited time

Other platforms, in addition to Airbnb, provide short-term rentals in Brooklyn. These rentals might be an excellent choice for families or bigger parties who prefer the privacy and convenience of their rooms. Websites like HomeAway and VRBO offer a wide range of possibilities, from apartments to townhouses and even waterfront properties.

When selecting your Brooklyn lodging, consider aspects such as location, budget, amenities, and personal preferences. Brooklyn has a broad choice of lodgings to pick from, whether you're looking for luxury or budget-friendly options.

Travel Budgeting Advice

Traveling to Brooklyn can be an exciting and memorable experience, but you must plan your vacation carefully to prevent overspending. You can make the most of your vacation to this busy borough without breaking the bank with a little preparation and cautious budgeting. Here are some money-saving suggestions to help you enjoy Brooklyn on a budget:

Accommodation

Accommodation is one of the most expensive aspects of traveling. Consider staying in budget-friendly choices such as hostels, guesthouses, or vacation rentals to save money. Brooklyn boasts a diverse choice of inexpensive hotels to suit all budgets. Airbnb and Booking.com provide numerous possibilities for low-cost vacationers.

Transportation

If you use the public transit system, you can get around Brooklyn for free. The subway is the most convenient and cost-effective way to commute inside the borough and around New York City. You can buy a MetroCard, which gives you unlimited trips for a set length of time or pay per ride. Walking or biking about Brooklyn is also an excellent way to see the neighborhoods while saving money on transportation.

Food

While Brooklyn is recognized for its rich food culture, dining out can rapidly add up. Consider investigating local markets and grocery stores where you can get cheaper fresh produce, snacks, and ready-to-eat meals. You can also try street food sellers or food trucks for inexpensive yet tasty lunches. Another alternative is to book lodgings with kitchens so you may prepare your meals.

Attractions for Free

Brooklyn has a wealth of free attractions and activities that allow you to explore the borough for free. Explore dynamic areas such as Williamsburg and DUMBO, or see classic monuments such as the Brooklyn Bridge and Prospect Park. Many Brooklyn museums and galleries also offer free entrance days or pay-what-you-wish admittance.

Entertainment at a Discount

If you want to visit paid attractions, check for discounted tickets or special offers. Popular Brooklyn activities, such as museums, tours, and entertainment venues, are frequently discounted on websites like Groupon. Consider visiting free events such as concerts, art exhibitions, or street festivals that are hosted throughout the year in Brooklyn.

Local Advice

Interacting with residents might provide useful tips on how to save money while enjoying the finest of Brooklyn. Request ideas from locals for inexpensive restaurants, hidden gems, and free or low-cost activities. Locals frequently know the best sites that tourists may not be aware of.

Timing

You can also save money by planning your trip to Brooklyn. Consider vacationing during the off-season, when hotel prices are typically lower. Furthermore, weekdays are less congested than weekends, which can lead to greater prices and discounts at attractions and restaurants.

Budget Preparation

Make a precise budget plan before your vacation to keep track of your costs. Set up money for lodging, transportation, food, attractions, and any miscellaneous expenses. This will assist you in sticking to your budget and avoiding overpaying.

Apps for Saving Money

Use money-saving applications that provide discounts, cashback incentives, or exclusive deals on a variety of services such as dining, transportation, and lodging. Apps like Groupon, Honey, and Traveloka can assist you in finding great deals and saving money when visiting Brooklyn.

Shopping for Souvenirs

Souvenirs in tourist destinations can be pricey. Instead of purchasing souvenirs from gift shops near major attractions, look for unusual and economical mementos of your vacation to

Brooklyn at small markets or independent boutiques.

You may have a fantastic trip in Brooklyn without breaking the bank if you follow these budgeting recommendations. Remember to plan ahead of time, look for low-cost solutions, and be open to discovering the borough's hidden jewels.

Information on Safety and Emergencies

Brooklyn, one of New York City's five boroughs, is a bustling and diversified destination with a diverse choice of activities and experiences for visitors. While Brooklyn is generally a safe area to visit, it is always a good idea to be informed of safety precautions and emergency information to have a pleasant and memorable vacation.

Precautions for Safety

General Security

When exploring Brooklyn, it is important to be cautious and aware of your surroundings, just as it is in any other urban location. Avoid exhibiting precious objects or carrying large sums of cash, and stick to well-lit and busy areas, especially at night.

Transportation by Public

Brooklyn has a well-developed public transit system that includes buses and subway lines. These modes of transportation are normally safe, however, you must be vigilant of your goods and keep them secure while traveling.

Road Safety

Always use authorized crosswalks and heed traffic signals when crossing roadways in Brooklyn. Vehicles, particularly bicycles and electric scooters, which are prominent sources of transportation in the borough, should be avoided.

Concern for the Community

Brooklyn is divided into neighborhoods, each with its distinct personality. While most neighborhoods are safe for visitors, it is a good idea to do some preliminary research on the place you intend to visit. Learn about local cultures, standards, and any relevant safety concerns.

Contact Persons in Case of Emergency

While visiting Brooklyn, it is critical to have emergency contact information readily available. In the United States, the general emergency number is 911, which can be contacted for quick assistance in the event of an emergency.

Services for Emergencies

Police

Brooklyn's major law enforcement agency is the New York City Police Department (NYPD). In the event of a criminal offense or an emergency needing police intervention, dial 911 or contact the nearest station directly.

Department of Fire

The New York City Fire Department (FDNY) is in charge of fire suppression and emergency medical services in the city. In the event of a fire or any other incident requiring quick assistance from the fire department, dial 911.

Medical Services

Brooklyn is home to several hospitals, clinics, and medical institutions that offer a variety of healthcare services. In the event of a medical emergency, phone 911 or go to the nearest hospital emergency department for immediate medical assistance.

Consulates and Embassies

If you are a foreign visitor and need assistance from your own country's embassy or consulate, keep their contact information handy. Most embassies and consulates provide emergency assistance to their nationals.

Natural Catastrophes

Brooklyn, like the rest of New York City, is vulnerable to natural calamities. While these incidents are uncommon, it is critical to be prepared and knowledgeable about potential hazards:

Hurricanes

Hurricanes have the potential to cause severe winds, heavy rain, and storm surges in Brooklyn. Keep up with weather updates and obey local authorities' instructions in the event of a hurricane warning or evacuation order.

Extreme Weather

Thunderstorms and severe weather are possible in Brooklyn. During such circumstances, it is best to stay indoors and follow the safety advice offered by local authorities.

Earthquakes

Although earthquakes are uncommon in the New York City area, they can occur. Learn earthquake safety precautions such as taking cover beneath strong furniture and staying away from windows during shocks.

Considerations for the Seasons

Brooklyn, one of New York City's five boroughs, endures dramatic seasonal changes throughout the year. Seasonal changes bring with them a variety of weather conditions and activities to enjoy in this dynamic and diversified borough. When organizing your activities in Brooklyn, whether you are a native or a guest, it is critical to consider the season. This travel guide includes detailed information on seasonal considerations in Brooklyn to help you make the most of your visit to this wonderful city.

Spring

Spring in Brooklyn is a lovely season when the borough blooms with flowers and trees. Temperatures range from mild to delightfully warm as the weather begins to warm up. It's a terrific time to visit Brooklyn's many parks and gardens, including Prospect Park, Brooklyn Botanic Garden, and Fort Greene Park, where you can see nature's rebirth. Picnics, biking, and leisurely walks along the waterfront promenades are among popular outdoor activities.

Summer

Summer in Brooklyn is hot and humid, with temperatures frequently reaching the upper 80s and lower 90s Fahrenheit (27-35 degrees Celsius). This time of year is ideal for taking advantage of the borough's numerous outdoor activities and events. During the summer, Coney

Island is a popular summer destination, with sandy beaches, amusement parks, and the famed boardwalk. Brooklyn Bridge Park offers breathtaking views of the Manhattan skyline as well as leisure activities such as kayaking and outdoor concerts. Throughout the summer, there are numerous street festivals, food markets, and cultural activities.

Fall

Autumn in Brooklyn is recognized for its vivid foliage, with leaves changing hues to red, orange, and yellow. Temperatures range from warm to chilly as the weather cools. It's a great time to explore Brooklyn's neighborhoods on foot or by bike while taking in the surroundings. Prospect Park provides stunning views of the fall foliage and holds events such as the annual

Halloween Parade. Other major events that take place during the fall season include the Brooklyn Book Festival and the DUMBO Arts Festival.

Winter

Winter in Brooklyn brings frigid temperatures that frequently reach below freezing, as well as snowfall. Despite the cold, there are still plenty of activities to enjoy this season. A favorite winter activity is ice skating at Prospect Park or the LeFrak Center in Lakeside. Throughout the winter, the Brooklyn Museum and the Brooklyn Academy of Music (BAM) host a variety of cultural activities and concerts. You can also warm up by visiting pleasant cafes, restaurants, and pubs that serve seasonal specialties.

Considerations All Year

Certain aspects should be considered when arranging a trip to Brooklyn at any time of year. To begin, it is recommended that you check the local weather prediction before your trip to pack proper attire and be prepared for any potential weather changes. Second, bear in mind that certain attractions or outdoor activities may have seasonal operating hours or closures, so check their websites or contact them directly for the most up-to-date information. Finally, public transit in Brooklyn is available all year and provides easy access to numerous areas and attractions.

Conclusion

As we conclude our tour of the borough of Brooklyn, we hope this travel guide has been a reliable companion, unlocking the doors to a world of discovery and delight. Brooklyn, with its rich history, various neighborhoods, and vibrant culture, is more than simply a destination; it's an experience that leaves an everlasting imprint on every visitor.

You've seen the multidimensional beauty that Brooklyn proudly possesses, from the iconic Brooklyn Bridge connecting the past to the present to the distinctive neighborhoods like Williamsburg and DUMBO that showcase the borough's artistic essence. The history, architecture, and people all contribute to the distinct and real appeal that characterizes this area of New York City.

We've walked you through the must-see attractions, culinary delights that excite the taste senses, and local experiences that capture the essence of Brooklyn life, as well as offer practical information to make your vacation as smooth as possible. Whether you explored Prospect Park's beautiful vegetation, sampled the different cuisines of Sunset Park, or danced the night away in Bushwick, we hope your adventures left you with lasting memories.

Remember that the tale of Brooklyn is ever-changing as you bid farewell. The tour may be over, but your connection to Brooklyn is not. Carry the essence of this dynamic place with you, where cultures meet, inventiveness has no limitations, and a strong feeling of community pervades.

Thank you for allowing us to be your tour guide through Brooklyn's streets. May your future journeys be filled with adventure, and may your memories of Brooklyn serve as a continual reminder of the borough's lively, ever-changing heartbeat. Happy travels until we meet again!

Made in the USA
Thornton, CO
07/27/24 19:38:45

7911c3e1-8863-4494-9d6c-41acb03b44d6R01